Mountain Strong: Patience in Practice

Islamic Leadership Institute of America

Youth Leadership Development Division

Ayman Nassar

Author: Ayman Nassar

Cover Design: Arif Kabir

Reviewers:
Hanem El-Shebini, Ph.D., Psychology & Social Studies, Trainer Mgmt Behavior
Illysa Izenberg, MBA, Faculty, University of Maryland (UMBC), Professional Studies
Mahmoud Abdelhady, Imam, Dar Al-Taqwa Masjid, Ellicott City, Maryland
Minhaj Hassan, Editor in Chief, The Muslim Link
Moataz Al-Hallak, Director, Muslim Community Association of Ann Arbor
Rascha Dughly, MD, Adult and Child Psychiatrist

Publisher: Intercontinental Networks Press, United States of America.

Copyright © 2009 Islamic Leadership Institute of America (ILIA).

All rights reserved. Printed in the United States of America. Except as permitted under the United States Copyright Act of 1976, no part of this publication may be reproduced or distributed in any form or by any means, or stored in a database or retrieval system, without prior written permission of the publisher.

First Edition, First Printing, July 2009 / Rajab 1430.

ISBN-10   0-9823685-8-5
ISBN-13   978-0-9823685-8-9

Copies of the book can be ordered through amazon.com, islamicleadership.org and other online bookstores. Bulk order discounts available by contacting ILIA Email: info@islamicleadership.org, Web: www.islamicleadership.org

Islamic Leadership Institute of America is a non-profit educational, research, charitable and religious organization dedicated to leadership, capacity and sustainability.

ILIA and Islamic Leadership Institute of America are trademarks of the Islamic Leadership Institute of America, Inc.

This book belongs to

Today's date is

All praises to the Lord of the Universe, Allah (praises and glory to Him), who perfected everything He created.

وَمَا خَلَقْتُ الْجِنَّ وَالْإِنسَ إِلَّا لِيَعْبُدُونِ

Al-Thariyat (51:56)

And I (Allah) created not the jinn and mankind except that they should worship Me (alone)

Meaning of Quranic Parable (51:56)

يَا أَيُّهَا الَّذِينَ آمَنُوا اصْبِرُوا وَصَابِرُوا وَرَابِطُوا وَاتَّقُوا اللَّهَ لَعَلَّكُمْ تُفْلِحُونَ

Al-Imran (3:200)

O you believers! Be patient in adversity, and vie in patience with one another, and be ever ready, and remain conscious of God, so that you may succeed.

Meaning of Quranic Parable (3:200)

Contents

WELCOME TO MOUNTAIN STRONG 9
ACKNOWLEDGMENTS 11
ISLAMIC LEADERSHIP INSTITUTE OF AMERICA 13
WARM UP 15
    A LITTLE BIT ABOUT YOURSELF 15
LEVELS OF PATIENCE 19
    WHAT IS PATIENCE? 20
    WHAT IS PERSEVERANCE? 28
    WHAT IS ENDURANCE? 30
    WHAT IS STEADFASTNESS? 32
HOW WILL PATIENCE BENEFIT ME? 35
    ALLAH'S SUPPORT 35
    LEADERSHIP 37
    GOODNESS 38
    PROTECTION 39
    STATUS 40
    SUCCESS 40
    LOVE 41
    GLAD TIDINGS 41
    STRENGTH 42
    BEST DEEDS 43
    BLESSINGS 43
    FORGIVENESS 44
    JANNAH 45
HOW CAN I BE PATIENT? 53
    PURIFICATION 53
    GOOD COMPANIONSHIP 54
    REMEMBRANCE OF ALLAH 55
    ACCEPTANCE 56
    VOLUNTEERING 57

   Modesty.. 58
      Live Your Age... 59
      Setting Goals... 60
      Complaining Only to Allah... 60
      Controlling Emotions... 61
      Balanced Life... 63

PRIME EXAMPLES OF PATIENCE 65

ARABIC TERMS 67

LEARN & READ MORE 71
   Hadith References.. 71
   Other References 72

ILIA LEADERSHIP DEVELOPMENT PROGRAMS............ 73
   General Available Programs 73
   Youth Leadership Development Programs....................................... 73

Welcome to Mountain Strong

Are you as strong as a mountain? Do you stand in the face of storms and quakes with strength and endurance? Do you hold on tight the same way the mountains hold down the continental plates?

Allah (glory be to Him) created the mountains strong, he made them withstand the challenges of the ages, erected high in the face of wind, rain, storms, or quakes. In the Quran, Allah (glory be to Him) describes the mountains as pegs that hold the crust of the earth from moving around, and keep the earth from shaking. Allah (glory be to Him) also explains that these mountains are strong and patient, yet humble to their creator.

There is no better place to experience patience than in the mountains, where we can reflect on Allah's creation and his magnificence. Indeed Allah (glory be to Him) has not created this earth in vain. Similarly there is no better source of knowledge for learning about patience than from the stories of the Prophets and messengers (peace and blessings be upon all of them), and the advice Allah (glory be to Him) has brought down to mankind in the Quran.

The Mountain Strong program, based on a mix of physical and intellectual activities, instills patience into youth. The team setting couples easy to intermediate levels of physical and academic games and activities, integrated with elements of responsibility and interdependence. This format ensures that 9-13 year old youth retain the concepts they experience during the program. Answers to the quizzes in this book are available at www.islamicleadership.org

Acknowledgments

الْحَمْدُ لِلَّهِ الَّذِي أَنزَلَ عَلَى عَبْدِهِ الْكِتَابَ وَلَمْ يَجْعَل لَّهُ عِوَجَا

Al-Kahf (18:1)

All praises and thanks are due to Allah, who has brought down the Book upon His servant, and has not allowed any deviousness in it.

Meaning of Quranic parable (18:1)

All praises to Allah (glory be to Him). Nothing in this book would have been possible without the bounties of Allah (glory be to him), of which guidance to Islam is the greatest bounties of all.

This book is the result of several people who contributed directly and indirectly, into making it an abridged reference for our youth in a format and language they can easily understand. Although it is developed with the intention to complement ILIA's leadership retreat "Mountain Strong: Patience into Practice", it could also be used independently.

Indeed as the Prophet (peace and blessings be upon him) has mentioned, whoever is not thankful to the people is not thankful to Allah,

Whoever does not thank the people is not thankful to Allah.

Prophet Muhammad Hadith [1]

Appreciation extends to my mother Hanem El-Shebini, Ph.D. Psychology; Rascha Dughly, MD, Adult and Child Psychiatrist; Minhaj Hassan, Editor-in-Chief, The Muslim Link; Imam Mahmoud Abdelhady, Imam of Dar Al-Taqwa, Maryland; Imam Moataz Al-Hallak, Director of the Muslim Community Association of Ann Arbor; and Illysa Izenberg, Leadership Faculty at the University of Maryland, Baltimore County, for their reviews and insights, on such a short notice. Their views represented a diverse range of domains from child development and psychology, to Islamic studies, media and leadership.

The driving force behind the Mountain Strong program was the motivation of Ammar Ibn Yasser and Arif Kabir. Their insights and vision drove this program, and inspired me to develop this book to accompany the activities. Arif designed an exceptional cover bringing a new dimension to the book.

It would be incomplete to not thank our youngsters Mohamed & Mostafa Halawa, Karim Mekkawy and Noor Bayomi for going through the book, and sharing their opinions on its effectiveness. I am also grateful to the members of the Islamic Writer Alliance, in particular Salim Hira, Leila Joiner and Linda Delgado for their suggestions related to Arabic fonts troubleshooting.

May Allah (glory be to Him) bless all the scholars of the past who carried the torch of knowledge and shared the insights this book presents, which is mostly based on Imam Shams Eldin Muhammad Ibn Abi Bakr Ibn Qayyim Al- Jawziyyah's book Uddat Al-Sabereen Wa Thakera Al-Shakereen عدة الصابرين وذخيرة الشاكرين.

Ibn Qayyim Al-Jawziyyah was born into a scholarly and virtuous family in 691 AH/ 1292 A.D. At that time Damascus was a center of knowledge and intellect. Many schools were located there and he studied and graduated under the protection, direction and sponsorship of his father. He was particularly influenced by his Shaykh and teacher Imam Ibn Taymiyyah, and also by Ibn Ash-Shirazi amongst others. Ibn Qayyim Al-Jawziyyah died in the city of Damascus the year 751 AH/1350 A.D., when he was almost 58 years old, and was buried at the cemetery of Bab Al-Saghir, near the grave of his father.

Islamic Leadership Institute of America

The Islamic Leadership Institute of America (ILIA), a not-for-profit organization founded in 2009, is a national institute solely dedicated to Islamic leadership, capacity and sustainability in North America. ILIA is a charitable, educational, research and religious organization addressing the need of strong leadership in Muslim communities and institutions.

ILIA builds institutional and individual leaders through youth leadership development, institutional sustainability development and community capacity building.

Our philosophy is based on Prophet Muhammad's statement (peace and blessings be upon him),

All of you are shepherds, and all of you are responsible for your flock

Prophet Muhammad Hadith [2]

We believe that our youth are not only the leaders of tomorrow, but also the leaders of today. In their schools, homes, and neighborhoods, our youth carry the same message that the youth of the cave carried thousands of years ago. They are self-leaders, leaders among their peers, siblings and families, and models for others to follow.

Leadership development starts from the early years of childhood, as the beloved Prophet (peace and blessings be upon him) mentions in the hadith to teach our children to pray at seven and to be disciplined for it at ten.

ILIA's Youth Leadership division focuses on the research, development, implementation and on-going realization of leadership traits, skills and knowledge in youth. The division is led by youth under the guidance of experienced professionals in leadership, management, psychology, child development, business, technology, education, Islamic studies and other domains.

This book is dedicated to all the youth who wish to make the best out of their teen years and build a solid foundation for their future. All proceeds from ILIA's youth programs go towards funding research and development work and activities in the area of youth leadership. Please purchase copies of this book as gifts for others to support ILIA's mission.

We dedicate this book to our younger brothers and sisters, and ask Allah (glory be to Him) to accept this work from us and to allow us to be part of sharing wisdom and enlightenment.

Ammar Ibn Yasser
Arif Kabir
Ayman Nassar
Salah Elleithy

Board of Directors
Islamic Leadership Institute of America
Rajab 28, 1430
July 20, 2009

Warm Up

A Little Bit About Yourself

Spend a few moments thinking about a few things that describe how you have dealt with challenges in the past. Your answers to the following questions will help you become a better leader. There are no right and wrong answers. Just answer the questions correctly to the best of your knowledge in the boxes on the right. When you see multiple answers on the right, just circle the one that makes the most sense.

How often do you have disagreements with one of your friends which turn into a problem?

| What is usually the cause for the disagreement? | |

| How do you think you can avoid the disagreement? | |

| How much do you like your school? | A lot – Somewhat – I don't |

| Why do you like it that much? | |

| What can you do to like your school more than you already do? | |

Do you get along with your siblings? | All the time - Some time - Never

If no, why not?

What does patience mean to you?

Do you consider yourself to be patient? | All the time - Some time - Never

Explain how you consider yourself to be patient.

Levels of Patience
Patience, Perseverance, Endurance and Steadfastness

يَا أَيُّهَا الَّذِينَ آمَنُواْ اصْبِرُواْ وَصَابِرُواْ وَرَابِطُواْ وَاتَّقُواْ اللَّهَ لَعَلَّكُمْ تُفْلِحُونَ

Al-Imran (3:200)

O you believers! Be patient in adversity, and vie in patience with one another, and be ever ready, and remain conscious of God, so that you may succeed.

Meaning of Quranic Parable (3:200)

What is Patience?

So what comes to your mind when you hear the word patience? Does it mean long hours, waiting, or boredom? Patience is actually a great blessing. People who are patient are successful, respected, live a peaceful and healthy life, and are from among the successful in the hereafter.

> To bear annoyance, pain, loss or anger without complaining.
>
> It is also to suppress anger, restlessness and complaining when confronted with a problem or loss.
>
> **Patience**

Imam Ibn Qayyim Al-Jawziyyah defined patience as the suppression and prevention; of the tongue from complaining, the soul from disappointment and the limbs from hitting and injuring when one is faced with a problem.

Are you a patient person? _____

Can you remember a time when you were patient? _____

Describe what happened and why you were patient

_____

_____

_____

_____

What made you patient?

_____

_____

_____

List two differences between the two patients below …

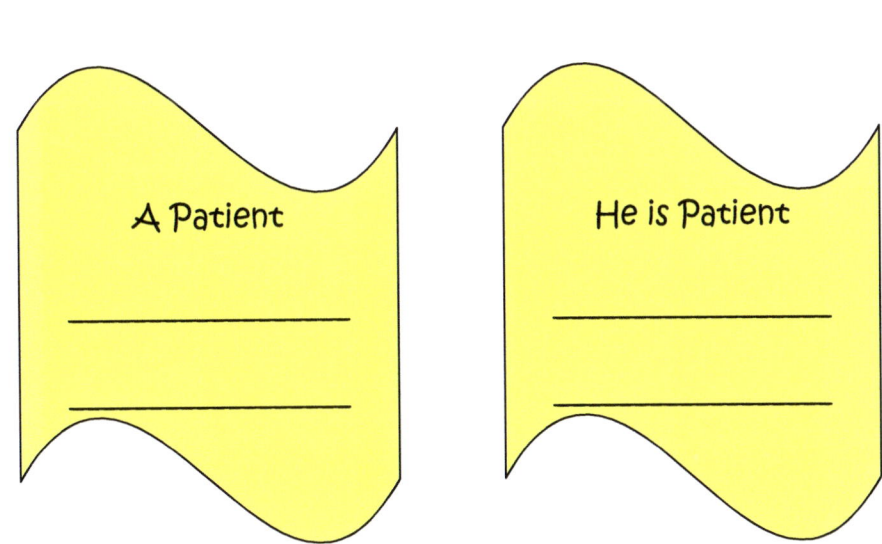

Now think of two similarities...

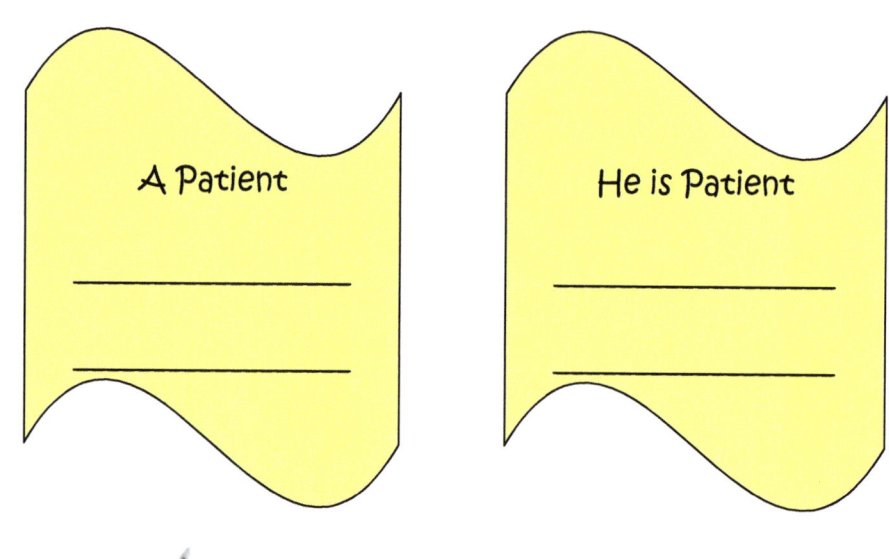

Describe a situation when you were not patient.

_____
_____
_____

How did you feel?

_____
_____
_____

What would you do differently now, to avoid being impatient again?

_____

_____

_____

Connect the words on the left with their synonyms on the right.

Patient   Passive

Disease   Cure

Treatment   Tolerance

Inactive   Sickness

Allah (glory be to Him) has ninety nine attributes that are authentic through confirmation in the Quran and Hadith.

We know that Allah (glory be to Him) has many names and attributes. He revealed some of his names and attributes in the Quran, and the Prophet (peace be upon him) taught us about the others through his hadiths. However there are many attributes that are kept unknown from mankind.

Which of the following names was not mentioned in the Quran?

Al-Saboor (The most patient) ☐

The only one who can ascribe to each affair an allotted order of timely occurrence according to His will and His ordinance. Nothing can cause any urgency to a decision, nor a change to a call for action before its elected time, and all things happen as predestined.

Al-Rahman (The most merciful) ☐

Implies both compassionate and forbearing treatment, especially of those who are weak, defenseless, powerless or those under severity. Allah is the Rahman in this life and the hereafter and the Raheem in the hereafter.

Al-Haleem (The most clement) ☐

He watches those who sin and disobey His commands, yet is not provoked to administer justice or inflict immediate punishment. He is the mild and gentle, and gives chances to his creation to submit and obey.

Some scholars consider Al-Saboor to be one of Allah's ninety nine names. The scholars which differ with them base their opinion on the fact that the term Al-Saboor was neither mentioned in the Quran nor in an authentic hadith. However, there are several hadiths that illustrate that Allah (glory be to Him) is the most patient, so there is no confusion that Allah (glory be to Him) is the most patient. It is just not considered one of the authentic names of Allah (glory be to Him).

The following hadith is an example that Allah (glory be to him) is the most patient. He is also the most clement, and both attributes are very close in meaning.

لا أحد أصبرُ على أذى يسمعه من الله عز وجل
إنه يُشْرَك به ويُجْعَل له الولد ثم هو يعافيهم ويرزقهم

None is more patient on hurting speech than Allah (glory be to Him). Associates and partners are made to Him, and statements are made about Him having a child. Yet, he gives them health and sustenance.

Prophet Muhammad Hadith [3]

Patience is a very important characteristic of a believer. People who are not patient always complain, are restless, shout, are perceived to be rude, and are not respected by others.

Examples of impatient people are panhandlers, kids who keep asking their parents over and over for the same thing, people who keep repeating the same instructions over and over and a manager who is always over the shoulders of his employees.

Panhandlers are impatient because they do not accept Allah's will for them to be less wealthy than others, and ask people for money without exerting any effort in working. Instead they should be thankful for what Allah has provided them with and seek to work or gain income in a lawful manner, through taking the means and exerting effort.

In Arabic patience is called sabr.

One day the Prophet (peace be upon him) passed by a graveyard, and he saw a women sitting next to a grave site who was initially wailing and screaming because her son had passed away. She then calmed down after a while. He told her to have taqwa and exhibit sabr – to fear Allah and be patient. She replied telling him to stay away from her. She told him that he has not been hit by a calamity like hers. She did not know that he was the Prophet. Later when she discovered that the man advising her was the Prophet, she went to his house to apologize. His response was "Indeed patience is at the first onset of a calamity."

Based on the story above, how would you act if after a long 6-hr hiking on a hot sunny and humid day, when you are starving and thirsty, your friend takes your water bottle and drinks it all?

    a. Take his bottle water and drink it all.

    b. Wait and think about why he took my bottle, and feel good about sharing.

    c. Twist his arm, or push him to the ground to get my bottle back.

As you jump into the lake for a swim your friends start calling you names and make fun of your skinny legs and arms. How do you react?

    a. Get out of the water and shout at them since they hurt my feelings.

    b. Go tell my friend Ahmed who is strong to beat them up.

    c. Get out of the lake sad and with a broken heart.

    d. Continue swimming not worried about what they are saying, and not responding to their remarks.

You made plans with your friends to meet at the masjid to pray Asr, and then play a football game on the green field behind the masjid. When you got to the masjid you found none of them. What would your first reaction be?

    a. Say to myself, these kids are useless and not serious people.

    b. Go to the Imam and complain to him that they did not keep their word and meet as agreed.

    c. Say glory be to Allah, and comfort myself by seeking excuses for their absence, and planning on making improvements so it does not repeat.

    d. Go home mad and never hang out with them again.

What is Perseverance?

Perseverance is similar to patience but involves continuous persistence in the face of obstacles or opposition.

For example, let's say that your teacher is giving out grades for an exam that you studied hard for. She then unexpectedly tells you that you got a C. In such a situation a patient student will not show signs of discontent or disapproval, but instead will accept the bad news with calmness. On the other hand, a student who not only shows acceptance, but also vows to study hard to get an A+ in the next exam, and then instead receives a B, and continues to have the intention to improve the grade and works hard to achieve the improved grade is not only patient, but also persistent and persevering despite all the challenges he or she is facing.

> To persist and continuously pursue a goal or objective despite continuous challenges and hardships that require patience.
>
> **Perseverance**

Imam Ibn Qayyim Al-Jawziyyah defined perseverance as patience when one is suffering the results of continuous patience.

In Arabic perseverance is known as ta'sabor.

Allah (glory be to Him) has created the angels with minds (they can think), but with no desires (they only worship Allah), and He (glory be to Him) created the animals and beasts with desires (they hunt, and reproduce), but with no ability to make distinctions. However humans were created by Allah (glory be to Him) with the ability to make choices and desires to control.

A believer who can control his desires by using good judgment of the mind, and exerting high levels of patience is acting as an angel. While on the other hand a believer whose desires overcome his patience is acting as an animal.

Which of the following is an example of patience?

a. Not getting angry because your parent told you not watch television.

b. Hiking for 15 miles in the hot sun in pain, with blisters on your feet and being bitten by insects and carrying a heavy backpack that has your supplies for the hike.

c. Waiting for your brother to finish talking on the phone for a few minutes so that you can make a call to your friend.

d. Sleeping during the day to avoid the hunger of fasting during Ramadan.

Which of the following is an example of perseverance?

a. Joining a group of cyclists on a 50 mile biking tour, getting tired, and enduring thirst and leg muscle pain after mile 30, and still insisting to continue for another three hours until the end of the bike trail.

b. Not getting mad after being bypassed in a lunch serving line three times while at school.

c. Playing with your three year old sister, while your mother prepares dinner, despite the fact you don't enjoy playing with dolls too much.

d. Doing your homework on time as your father advised you to do.

What is Endurance?

Endurance is the act of going through very hard suffering to prevent a great harm, or loss.

An example of endurance is when someone attacks you and your family in your home, and you patiently defend yourself, persevere and endure the pain of the physical attack, and stay firm to defend yourself and family without giving up. Several words that reflect the meaning of endurance are tenacity, never giving up, dying while trying and unfaltering.

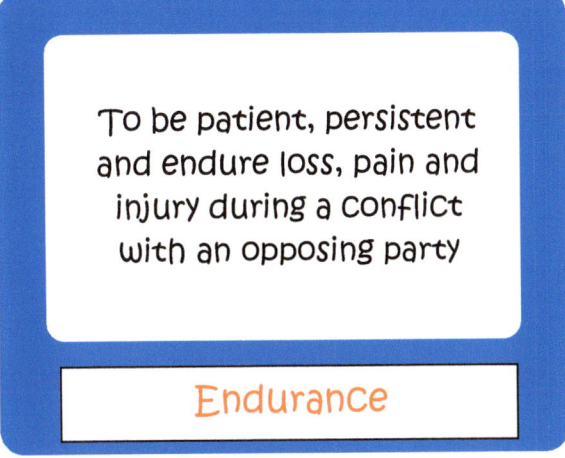

To be patient, persistent and endure loss, pain and injury during a conflict with an opposing party

Endurance

In Arabic endurance is known as mo'sabara

Imam Ibn Qayyim Al-Jawziyyah defines patience as one's state with oneself, while endurance is one's state with another party. This means that when we are patient in a matter that involves another party and both parties are competing in a matter, or there is mutual perseverance and challenge, the level of patience required is higher is known as endurance.

Connect the words on the left with their situations on the right.

Patience — Ahmed helps his dad with painting a room in the house. Each time he paints a part of the wall, he drips paint on the floor, but yet pauses to place the paint brush on the tray and wipe the dripping paint off the floor.

Endurance — Amr was standing in the long line at the museum to buy tickets for a show for his younger sister, not complaining about the wait and tired he is.

Perseverance — Sabbi getting bad-mouthed by his friends at school because he prays Thuhr prayer on time everyday, and does not have any girl friends. Sometimes they even call him names, push him in the school hallway, and don't talk to him during lunch and recess.

What is Steadfastness?

The definition of steadfastness is the act of staying firmly fixed in place, and firm in belief, determined and adhering to one's belief or position.

In Arabic the word steadfast is known as mo'ra'ba'ta.

المُرابطة

To be steadfast one has to be patient and able to persevere and endure.

One common example is pushing back against peer pressure at school. Sometimes your friends at school will say things that hurt your feelings. These hurtful comments could be about the way you dress, worship, walk, talk, or anything that affects you personally. By being patient, you will make sure that you are not affected by what they say, and by persevering, you will always remain patient and not lose your temper. Endurance will help you take the emotional harm they inflict on you and not give in to peer pressure. If you are steadfast, you will be able to not only get through the bullying or harsh comments, but also stand strong with your ideals, and even share them with others, including those harming you.

Here is an example of being steadfast, when sister Heba was in 6th grade, a boy made fun of her scarf, he told her she must be bald to wear a rag on her head. She was patient and would respond with manners and wisdom. He repeated it over and over, and each time she would just be patient and wise. The boy finally got frustrated with her patience and perseverance, so he started to spread rumors about her hair and appearance. He even went on to speculate that covering her hair had to do with being a slow thinker. Other people in the class started treating her harshly and made fun of her in science projects and team assignments, yet she persevered. Each time she made a statement on a team project and her peers made fun of her, she would get stronger and make another suggestion; never brought down by their immature comments. One day another girl who was jealous of Heba tried to trip her during the P.E. class, but Heba endured the stress and hardship her peers would impose on her. She was steadfast and when it was time for the "International Day" school fair a few months later, she got permission from her teacher to do a project on Islam, to educate her peers on hijab, modesty and humbleness.

She was steadfast and stuck to her Islamic beliefs and was successful because it all started with her patience.

A lesson we gain from this short story, is that no matter what we go through in life, we will always face challenges. Some challenges will be small, others will be big. Only strong men will pass these challenges, and men can only be strong through patience, perseverance, endurance and steadfastness.

> Never let go of controlling you anger ….
>
> Never give up, no matter how many times you fail ….
>
> Never give in, pain will pay off at the end …..
>
> Never break down, stand tall, calling for truth ….

It is important to differentiate between passivity and endurance. To endure does not mean to be passive, but rather to overcome challenges striving for a bigger goal, and actively taking the means.

How Will Patience Benefit Me?

Support, Leadership, Goodness .... and Jannah

Allah's Support

In the Quran, Allah mentions that if we are to be patient, he will help us out and support us. This is stated in the chapter of Al-Anfal below.

$$\text{وَأَطِيعُواْ اللَّهَ وَرَسُولَهُ وَلاَ تَنَازَعُواْ فَتَفْشَلُواْ وَتَذْهَبَ رِيحُكُمْ وَاصْبِرُواْ إِنَّ اللَّهَ مَعَ الصَّابِرِينَ}$$

Al-Anfal (8:46)

And obey Allah and His messenger, and do not dispute and with one another, lest you fail and your strength departs, and have patience. Indeed Allah is with those who are patient.

The Spoils of War (8:46)

Patience means to accept Allah's will and ordinance. When we become impatient, we are acting in a way as if we are rebellious towards Allah (glory be to Him). Impatience is an expression of not being content with what Allah (glory be to Him) has decreed. Allah (glory be to Him) will not support or aid a rebellious servant.

It is very easy for us to lose patience when we have disagreements with each other. Take for example the situation where you and your friends are playing football; you start to dispute who should be on which team, and the dispute grows larger. As the discussion gets heat up, team members lose interest in playing, and don't feel motivated any more to be part of the game. Eventually, instead of playing with a team that one might not want to be part of, the argument ends with no game being played at all.

It is important to be smart and never let Shaytan or any other enemy make us dispute among ourselves. We need to always look at the bigger picture and remember that we are all brothers serving Allah (glory be to Him), and because of that, we have to be patient with any disagreements or differences we come across.

Remember the story of Prophet Younis (peace be upon him), and how he lost patience in sharing the message of Allah, when none of his society would believe in Allah's message. Younis (peace be upon him) lost hope, and stopped calling people to the way of Allah. As a result of his lack of patience, Allah (glory be to Him) tested him and took his support away from him, he let him get thrown into the ocean and swallowed by the whale. It was only when Younis (peace be upon him) was in the whale's abdomen that he realized he had not been patient and had been a transgressor. At that moment Younis (peace be upon him) called upon Allah to forgive him, and only then, Allah forgave him, and brought him out of the whale's abdomen.

Have you been in a situation before, where you disputed or argued with someone and as a result you both become less effective?

_____

_____

_____

Leadership

Patience brings leadership to those who practice it. Allah (glory be to Him) talks about the group of believers who were made leaders by Allah (glory be to Him) sharing guidance with others and encouraging the command of Allah (glory be to Him), as a result of their patience and deep belief in Allah's signs. This is reflected in the chapter of Al-Sajdah.

وَجَعَلْنَا مِنْهُمْ أَئِمَّةً يَهْدُونَ بِأَمْرِنَا لَمَّا صَبَرُوا وَكَانُوا بِآيَاتِنَا يُوقِنُونَ

Al-Sajdah (32:24)

And We raised among them leaders who, guided their people with Our command, so long as they carried themselves with patience and had sure faith in Our parables.

Meaning of Quranic Parable (32:24)

Goodness

Imagine having goodness all the time. Imagine Allah giving you goodness whenever you have a situation that is not pleasant. You can get goodness in this life and the hereafter each time you face something you don't like or are asked to do something you don't enjoy.

In the chapter of the Bee in the Quran, Allah tells us that if we are to be patient, it will be better for us.

وَلَئِن صَبَرْتُمْ لَهُوَ خَيْرٌ لِّلصَّابِرِينَ

Al-Nahl (16:126)

And to bear yourselves with patience is indeed far better for those who are patient in adversity.

Meaning of Quranic Parable (16:126)

This part of the verse follows a statement by Allah commanding mankind to enforce justice through implementing a punishment that is equivalent to the aggression that took place. Allah (glory be to Him) then advises us, that if we are to forgive and have patience, that is even better in the eyes of Allah, and we will be rewarded more goodness.

For example, if you are pushed at school by another student, you can report it to the school principal. The principal can order the other student to be suspended, or you can ask the principal to forgive him, and if you do that, there will be more good for you as a result of your patience.

Protection

Patience brings protection by Allah (glory be to Him), as long as our patience is pure for the sake of Allah (glory be to Him), and our hearts are pure and have good intentions. Allah (glory be to Him) explains this in the Quran in the chapter of the Family of Imran.

$$\text{وَإِن تَصْبِرُواْ وَتَتَّقُواْ لاَ يَضُرُّكُمْ كَيْدُهُمْ شَيْئًا إِنَّ اللّهَ بِمَا يَعْمَلُونَ مُحِيطٌ}$$

Al-Nahl (16:126)

And if you are patient in adversity and conscious of Allah, their evil plotting cannot harm you at all: for, verily, Allah encompasses all that they do.

Meaning of Quranic Parable (16:126)

Allah (glory be to Him) tells us that if we are patient and purified, then the plots against us of those who do not like us will not succeed, and that Allah is all aware of their actions and evil deeds.

I am sure that you know the story of Prophet Ibrahim (Abraham) peace be upon him. His people plotted to throw him into the fire as a punishment to his calling to the way of Allah. Ibrahim had patience in Allah's test and had a heart that was pure of any shortcomings. As a result Allah (glory be to Him) commanded the fire to be cold and peace on Ibrahim, and he was saved.

Status

Do you remember the story of Prophet Youssef (peace be upon him), and how he was betrayed by his brothers, sold in the market as a slave, and then imprisoned falsely? Youssef, however, had patience, and as a result, Allah (glory be to Him) gave him high status in the society, and he was eventually the leader of Egypt. Allah (glory be to Him) shares this story with us in the Quran in the chapter of Joseph.

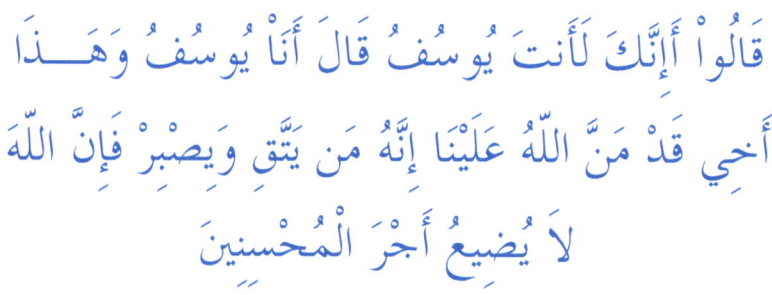

Youssef (12:90)

They exclaimed: Is it indeed that you are Joseph? He answered: "I am Joseph, and this is my brother. God has indeed been gracious unto us. Verily, if one is conscious of Him and patient in adversity behold, God does not waste the deeds of those who perfect their deeds.

Meaning of Quranic Parable (12:90)

Success

Patience is one of the ingredients to success. In the chapter of the Family of Imran, which is the family of Mary (peace be upon her), Allah (glory be to Him) illustrates the various levels of controlling one's self and bearing hardship.

$$\text{يَا أَيُّهَا الَّذِينَ آمَنُوا اصْبِرُوا وَصَابِرُوا وَرَابِطُوا وَاتَّقُوا اللَّهَ لَعَلَّكُمْ تُفْلِحُونَ}$$

Al-Imran (3:200)

O you believers! Be patient in adversity, and vie in patience with one another, and be ever ready, and remain conscious of God, so that you may succeed.

Meaning of Quranic Parable (3:200)

Love

This might sound a bit surprising, but yes, you can gain love by being patient. The love of Allah (glory be to Him) is the greatest love of all. Whomever Allah loves will be loved by those who love Allah (glory be to Him). In other words, if you gain Allah's love, He will make people who are righteous and pious love you. Look at what Allah (glory be to Him) says about the believers who are patient.

Al-Imran (3:146)

And Allah loves those who are patient in adversity

Meaning of Quranic Parable (3:146)

Glad Tidings

Each one of us goes through some very difficult times, or calamities. Some of us might have experienced these difficult situations, like losing a parent or grandparent, our father losing his job, or a close relative getting very sick. All of these difficult situations are big tests from Allah (glory be to Him) which give us a chance to prove to ourselves and Allah (glory be to Him) how content we are with His ordinance, and how patient we are.

وَلَنَبْلُوَنَّكُم بِشَيْءٍ مِّنَ الْخَوْفِ وَالْجُوعِ وَنَقْصٍ مِّنَ الْأَمْوَالِ وَالْأَنفُسِ وَالثَّمَرَاتِ وَبَشِّرِ الصَّابِرِينَ

Al-Baqara (2:155)

And most certainly shall We test you through danger, hunger, and loss of worldly goods, of lives and of fruits. But give glad tidings to those who are patient in adversity.

Meaning of Quranic Parable (2:155)

Strength

Patience makes us strong believers, both physically and spiritually. It is an aid to us in our duties and obligations, and it makes us overcome obstacles. One example Allah (glory be to Him) gives in the Quran is using patience and prayers to gain strength to perform our worship obligations. This is discussed in the chapter of the Cow.

وَاسْتَعِينُواْ بِالصَّبْرِ وَالصَّلَاةِ وَإِنَّهَا لَكَبِيرَةٌ إِلَّا عَلَى الْخَاشِعِينَ

Al-Baqara (2:45)

And seek aid in steadfast patience and prayer: and this, indeed, is a hard thing for all but the humble in spirit.

Meaning of Quranic Parable (2:45)

Best Deeds

One of the best deeds a believer can do is being patient. Imam Ibn Qayyim Al-Jawziyyah describes belief as two halves. The first half is patience and the second is thankfulness. It is true that a deed cannot have the sincere intention if the believer is not thankful to Allah and not patient with Allah's will.

Allah tells us in the Quran that whoever is patient and forgiving, then indeed his deeds are from among the best of deeds.

وَلَمَن صَبَرَ وَغَفَرَ إِنَّ ذَلِكَ لَمِنْ عَزْمِ الْأُمُورِ

Al-Shura (42:43)

And if one is patient in adversity and forgives - this, behold, is indeed something from among the best of recommendations by Allah.

Meaning of Quranic Parable (42:43)

Blessings

Allah (glory be to Him) showers the believers who have patience with mercy and compassion and bestows upon them His blessings.

Allah (glory be to Him) is the most merciful and most compassionate, and always gives us hope. He gives the believers glad tidings that if they are affected by a calamity, and they are patient, He will shower them with his mercy and tranquility, and make them from among the truly guided. This is stated in the chapter of the Cow in the Quran.

$$\text{أُولَـٰئِكَ عَلَيْهِمْ صَلَوَاتٌ مِّن رَّبِّهِمْ وَرَحْمَةٌ وَأُولَـٰئِكَ هُمُ الْمُهْتَدُونَ}$$

Al-Baqara (2:157)

It is they upon whom their Sustainer's blessings and grace are bestowed, and it is they, they who are on the right path!

Meaning of Quranic Parable (2:157)

Forgiveness

All believers strive for the forgiveness of Allah (glory be to Him). Regardless of how good we perfect our actions, we will still have shortcomings; the acts of worship performed will not be at a level that meets Allah's (glory be to Him) magnificence.

Allah (glory be to Him) gives us good news in the Quran that he forgives the believers who are patient and do good deeds, and grants them an immense reward.

$$\text{إِلَّا الَّذِينَ صَبَرُواْ وَعَمِلُواْ الصَّالِحَاتِ أُوْلَـٰئِكَ لَهُم مَّغْفِرَةٌ وَأَجْرٌ كَبِيرٌ}$$

Al-Baqara (2:157)

Most people except for those who are patient in adversity and do righteous deeds: it is they whom forgiveness of sins awaits, and a great reward.

Meaning of Quranic Parable (2:157)

Jannah

Our ultimate goal as believers is to eternally dwell in jannah and be pleased by Allah (glory be to Him). This also can be attained through patience, as Allah reveals in the wonderful chapter of The Believers.

$$إِنِّي جَزَيْتُهُمُ الْيَوْمَ بِمَا صَبَرُوا أَنَّهُمْ هُمُ الْفَائِزُونَ$$

Al-Muminun (23:111)

Indeed, today I have rewarded them for their patience in adversity: verily, it is they, they who have achieved triumph and success.

Meaning of Quranic Parable (23:111)

This parable in the Quran is a very comforting one for the believers who have been patient during their life-times, striving for the pleasure of their Lord. In humbleness they would accept what Allah has given them, and in humility they would ask Allah (glory be to Him) for more. These patient believers are the ones who did not complain about hardships, nor did they lose hope in Allah's mercy and love.

As youth we always need to be thankful to Allah (glory be to Him) for what He has given us. He blessed us with the greatest of blessings; the blessing of Islam; that is the blessing of following the truth, and submitting to our Lord, Allah, hence He named us Muslims which means the submitters.

Our submission is part of our patience. The patience in conducting our acts of worship on time and as commanded; the patience in staying away from sin and evil; the patience in doing

> Patience in what we have to do
> > Patience in fulfilling the acts of worship …
> > Patience in commanding and doing good …..
>
> Patience in what we should not do
> > Patience in staying away from sin and evil ….
> > Patience in disliked matters in Islam ….
> > Patience in questionable issues….
>
> Patience in what is happening to you
> > Patience in calamities and hardships ….
> > Patience in forgiving others …
> > Patience in doing something we don't enjoy …

things we might not enjoy to come closer to Allah; the patience in hardships; and the patience in obeying Allah's commands, are all components of a believing young Muslim's patience.

We can group the different types of patience into three main groups. The first of the three is a group of things *we must do*, like acts of worship and obeying Allah, preventing evil and staying away from sin. The second group comprises of things *we must not do*, such as sinning, disobeying Allah and committing haram. The final group involves things that *we go through* such as losing a loved one, being harmed by another person or going through some though challenges in life.

Acts of worship include not associating other priorities with Allah, praying on time, fasting, giving charity, respecting the parents, following the Quran and making duaa to Allah. These are just some acts of worship from among many other forms of worship.

Commanding good includes sharing the message of Islam with others, advising one's friends to do good deeds, teaching the Quran to others, removing harm from one's way, and many other good deeds.

Being truthful, having good friends, using only good language, not being arrogant, and not talking about others in their absence are all examples of staying away from sin and evil.

Disliked matters in Islam, are also known as mak.roo.h. These are matters that if one gets involved in he will not be punished, but staying away from them will grant one good deeds. Examples are growing long nails, excess sleep, divorce and delaying washing from a state of janaba.

Questionable issues are issues which are not clearly haram nor halal, and staying away from these issues is required, so that one does not fall into the haram. When Allah (glory be to Him) speaks about haram in the Quran, he commands us to not even come close to it. One example is when Allah told Adam and his wife to not come close to the tree in the jannah. Another example is when Allah orders us to not come close to fornication and adultery.

Imagine that there are three pieces of land adjacent to each other, one on the right and the other on the left. The piece of land on the right has only halal activities and events taking place, while the one on the left only has haram activities and events. The land in the middle has activities that are neither halal nor haram, but are mubah, meaning neutral. As a Muslim you can go all the way to the border of the halal. If you pass the border you will enter the neutral land, which is neither going to reward you for a deed, nor result in a sin. However as you move further towards the left approaching the border between the mubah land and the haram land, you risk crossing into the haram land without noticing, in which case you will accumulate sins and bad deeds. For this reason it is always required that we stay as far possible as we can from the border with the haram land, and this means that we stay away from disliked and questionable issues to the best of our abilities.

When Allah (glory be to Him) talks about haram issues he commands us to stay away from them, and not even come close to these haram issues. An example is below; the first example gives us a glimpse of the story of Adam (peace be upon Him) when Allah (glory be to Him) commands him to stay away from the tree in the jannah. Allah not only commanded that Adam not eat from the tree, but instead commanded Adam to stay away from the tree completely.

وَقُلْنَا يَا آدَمُ اسْكُنْ أَنتَ وَزَوْجُكَ الْجَنَّةَ وَكُلاَ مِنْهَا رَغَداً حَيْثُ شِئْتُمَا وَلاَ تَقْرَبَا هَـذِهِ الشَّجَرَةَ فَتَكُونَا مِنَ الْظَّالِمِينَ

Al-Baqara (2:35)

And We said: "O Adam, dwell thou and thy wife in this garden, and eat freely thereof, both of you, whatever you may wish; but do not approach this one tree, lest you become wrongdoers."

Meaning of Quranic Parable (2:35)

Connect the types of patience on the left with their situations on the right …

Patience in fulfilling the acts of worship	Not listening to nasheeds that have music
Patience in doing something we might not enjoy	Getting up early every day to join my dad at Fajr prayer at the masjid
Patience in commanding and doing good	Not cursing my friend back
Patience in obeying Allah's command	Doing homework on time
Patience in forgiving others	Helping brother Ahmed with cleaning his backyard instead of playing football with my friends
Patience in calamities and hardships	Not cursing if my PSP gets stolen
Patience in questionable issues	Not complaining about my parents not letting me go out with my friends
Patience in staying away from sin and evil	Not talking about others from behind their backs
Patience in staying away from sin	Not using bad language to express boredom when staying home bored in bed after an operation

Which of the following patience types are mandatory and which are recommended?

Patience in fulfilling the acts of worship _____

Patience in staying away from sin and evil _____

Patience in commanding and doing good _____

Patience in calamities and hardships _____

Patience in forgiving others _____

Patience in disliked matters _____

Patience in questionable issues _____

Did you know that some forms of patience are haram? Can you guess which of the following forms of patience are haram, disliked, recommended or mandatory? (Put an H in the box, if haram, D if disliked, R if recommended, and M if mandatory)

Not eating a dead animal while lost in the woods leading to death by starvation ☐

Not protecting oneself from beasts or reptiles ☐

Avoiding high thrill amusement park rides that could potentially harm one ☐

Not eating until one feels dizzy or weak ☐

Not staying up late at night, to be able to get up early for Fajr ☐

Not having ill feelings because dad said I cannot spend the night at my friend's house ☐

How Can I Be Patient?
Purification, Companionship, Remembrance...

Sometimes we lose control of our emotions or limbs, and our desires can make us impatient. Allah (glory be to Him) gave us some great advice to help us build our patience. Several key tips from the Quran are mentioned in this chapter.

Purification

Purification is the process of cleaning one's self from sins and evil. Purification should be done to the soul, body, and one's property. For example, purification of the soul can occur by fasting, praying, making duaa, and remembering Allah. Purification of the body occurs through wudu and showering. Purification of the wealth occurs through paying zakat and charity.

Allah (glory be to Him) tells us in the Quran that fasting has been prescribed upon us to purify us. Fasting involves preventing one from his or her desires. During fasting, one is not allowed to eat, drink, use foul language, back-bite people, lie, be deceptive, or cause any harm or evil. By constantly recognizing that one is fasting and repeating the process every day during Ramadan for thirty days, a believer can develop patience and perseverance.

Similarly, by giving away what might be dear to us like some of one's wealth to the poor and needy we can develop patience.

Good Companionship

The chapter of the Cave shares one of the beautiful stories of the past. It is the story of the young men who were patient and steadfast against the tyrant ruler of the land. The ruler killed all those who opposed him and worshipped Allah. These young men were patient and endured the harms of the ruler. They used their intellect to find means to escape his tyranny, until one day they found a cave where they entered to rest. Because of their belief and patience, Allah gave them mercy by putting them to sleep for three hundred and nine years, so that they would not suffer from the ruler and would be saved.

In the chapter of the Cave, Allah (glory be to Him) tells the believers to seek patience by being around believers who remember Allah in the morning and night.

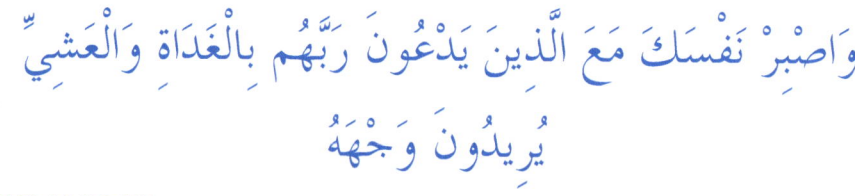

Al-Kahf (18:28)

And have patience in yourself by being with those who at morning and at evening call upon their Lord, seeking His pleasure.

Meaning of Quranic Parable (18:28)

Following this advice is to be friends with people who are humble, remember Allah, and are aware of their actions. We should not associate ourselves or be friends with people who do not worry if Allah will punish them or not, or people who do not remember why they were created or what Allah commands them to do. Only when we are surrounded by people who remember the Creator, Sustainer and Provider of the universe, will we be content, happy and patient.

Remembrance of Allah

Remembering Allah (glory be to Him) is a great way to be patient. This is because each time we do something good we will remember Allah's blessings and rewards, so we will do it even better and spend more time and effort on perfecting it to please Him further. This extra dedication will help us build our patience.

On the other hand, remembering Allah (glory be to Him) when one is doing a bad deed, will make him stop it and fear the consequences, which is another form of patience and self-discipline.

Allah (glory be to Him) says in the Quran that it is through remembering Allah that the hearts of the believers become content and satisfied, as a result patience will be manifested.

$$\text{الَّذِينَ آمَنُوا وَتَطْمَئِنُّ قُلُوبُهُم بِذِكْرِ اللَّهِ أَلَا بِذِكْرِ اللَّهِ تَطْمَئِنُّ الْقُلُوبُ}$$

Al-Ra'ad (13:28)

Those who believe, and whose hearts find their rest in the remembrance of Allah, for, verily, in the remembrance of Allah hearts do find their rest.

Meaning of Quranic Parable (13:28)

Acceptance

As long as we recognize that Allah (glory be to Him) is the most capable and the most merciful, we assure ourselves that he will never let us down, or stop supporting us, as long as we are sincere in our belief and reflect this sincerity in our actions and knowledge.

Allah gave great advice to the beloved Prophet Muhammad to not worry about the harm he was receiving from the disbelievers of Makkah, as they mocked him and called him a crazy poet or witch and to have patience in the command of Allah, and His will.

$$\text{وَاصْبِرْ لِحُكْمِ رَبِّكَ فَإِنَّكَ بِأَعْيُنِنَا وَسَبِّحْ بِحَمْدِ رَبِّكَ حِينَ تَقُومُ}$$

Al-Tur (52:45)

And await in patience your Lord's judgment, for you are well within Our sight. And praise and thank your Lord whenever you rise and establish.

Meaning of Quranic Parable (52:45)

We also learn from this ayah that praising Allah (glory be to Him) at different occasions such as getting ready for prayer, waking up in the morning, or leaving a gathering is a characteristic of a patient person who always remembers his Lord.

Volunteering

The Prophet (peace be upon him) always encouraged the companions to interact with people who were less capable in the society to strengthen their appreciation of the bounties Allah (glory be to Him) has bestowed upon them.

Serving the needs of the people on a volunteer basis, not seeking any benefit in this dunya, is a great way to develop patience. This is mainly due to the fact that there is no worldly benefit, and the only driver is good will and serving others to gain the pleasure of Allah (glory be to Him).

Youth have time available during school breaks and on weekends which they could use to feed the hungry at soup kitchens, serve the homeless at local shelters, support their communities at the masjid and visit the sick and orphans. There is a long list of things you can do to develop patience, here are a few.

- Memorize the Quran, a few ayat every day.
- Cut the grass for an elder neighbor instead of watching TV.
- Plant flowers and seeds early in spring to observe them bloom and grow throughout the summer.
- Sow and till a piece of land to grow some vegetables to experience how much work it takes to prepare the land, clear it from weeds, seed it, and then keep it healthy and clear of weeds.

- Help your parents with errands at home, like organizing and folding the laundry.
- Read to a younger sibling.
- Develop a hobby that reflects on Allah's creation (bird watching, chemistry experiments, rock collection).
- Volunteer at soup kitchen, shelters, masjids, or orphanages.

Modesty

Allah (glory be to Him) tested Prophet Ayoub (Peace be upon him) with a severe calamity. He was rich and strong, had many children, about ten, and was a very popular and well-known man in his society. One day Allah (glory be to Him) struck him with an illness that made his skin peel off. It was so severe to the extent that people avoided him, and one day his wife went to the market place to buy items, and when she came back home, she could not recognize Prophet Ayoub. Not only he became sick and was avoided by the people, but also he lost all his children and lost his wealth.

Although Ayoub's life turned into a miserable experience, he was content. Whenever his wife would ask him to make duaa to Allah (glory be to Him) to cure him, he would respond saying that Allah has given him so much in the past that he feels humble to ask Allah for cure and recovery.

After many requests from his wife to make duaa to Allah, Ayoub made this sincere and modest duaa, instead of asking Allah (glory be to Him) for cure, he just stated in humbleness his condition to Allah (glory be to Him) and asked Allah (glory be to Him) for his mercy through any means.

وَأَيُّوبَ إِذْ نَادَىٰ رَبَّهُ أَنِّي مَسَّنِيَ الضُّرُّ وَأَنتَ أَرْحَمُ الرَّاحِمِينَ

Al-Anbiya (21:83)

And Job, when he cried out to his Sustainer, "Affliction has befallen me: but Thou art the most merciful of the merciful!"

Meaning of Quranic Parable (21:83)

Live Your Age

Many young people feel eager to grow up quickly, and to participate in activities of their older siblings or neighbors. While it is beneficial for youngsters to learn from older role models, it is important to know that each age group has its interests and abilities. Many times when youth participate in discussions or activities with older peers, it causes distraction and confusion. It is becoming all too common to witness pre-teens who are not interested in their age activities, and instead feel the urge to grow up quickly and participate in older teens' activities.

A common piece of advice I hear from many inmates who fell into trouble at a young age is to tell the youth to live their age. A twelve year old should engage in activities of a twelve year old and not a sixteen year old.

If you don't live your age now, you will never live it, simply because it will never come back. We are ten only when we are ten, and twelve only when we are twelve. So live your life and don't hasten; indeed Allah has plans, and when the right time comes for these plans, He will make them happen.

Setting Goals

Goals are things we look forward and strive to achieve; for example, being on the basketball team which will compete at the state finals. To be able to achieve these goals, they need to be clear and specific. It is always a good idea to write your goals down in a notepad and think about them carefully. Also your goals should be realistic, which means they are neither imaginary, nor unpractical. If someone never played basketball in their life, it will be unreasonable to expect they join a national team in a few weeks of practice.

The Prophet (peace be upon him) encouraged us to set goals and work for our life in this dunya, as if we will never pass away; and to set goals and work for our hereafter as if we will pass way tomorrow. This advice tells us that we need to balance our goals. As young people we need to have religious, educational and social goals among many others.

Complaining Only to Allah

The believer should only complain to Allah (glory be to Him). We realize that Allah is the most capable and in full control of everything. We have full belief that Allah will take care of our affairs as long as we are sincere and truthful in our submission to Him. When a believer needs support, the first thing one should do is to make duaa to Allah (glory be to Him), and ask for Allah's support. A believer must take the means of accomplishing activities, including the resolution of problems, and this could include consultation with others, but we only complain and seek assistance from Allah.

A great example of complaining to Allah (glory be to Him) is Prophet Yaqub's (peace be upon him) grieving, when he missed his son Youssef (peace be upon him). When told by his other children that he would never forget Youssef until he grew old and weak, or died, Yaqub replied:

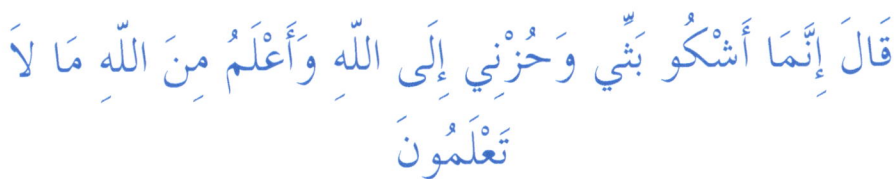

Youssef (12:86)

He answered: "It is only to Allah that I complain of my deep grief and my sorrow: for I know, from Allah, something that you do not know

Meaning of Quranic Parable (12:86)

Controlling Emotions

The Prophet (peace and blessings be upon him) always controlled his emotions. When something would make the Prophet upset, he would suppress his anger. The Prophet would never raise his voice or be rude to anyone, even if the person harmed the Prophet. The Prophet used to have a non-Muslim neighbor who would place human waste and filth in front of the Prophet's house every day. One day the neighbor did not place any new filth in front of the Prophet's home, and this repeated a few times in sequence. The Prophet then got worried about his neighbor and went to visit his neighbor. This is an example of how the Prophet not only held his anger and controlled his emotions, but also extended his kindness to his neighbor.

There are many other great examples of how Prophets controlled their anger, such as that of Yaqub when his children reminded him of Youssef; he suppressed his sorrow as noted in the ayah in the chapter of Youssef.

$$\text{وَتَوَلَّىٰ عَنْهُمْ وَقَالَ يَا أَسَفَىٰ عَلَىٰ يُوسُفَ وَابْيَضَّتْ عَيْنَاهُ مِنَ الْحُزْنِ فَهُوَ كَظِيمٌ}$$

Youssef (12:85)

And he turned away from them and said, my grief for Youssef, and he lost his sight because of his sorrow that he was suppressing

Meaning of Quranic Parable (12:86)

When Prophet Muhammad's son Ibrahim passed away, the companions noticed he had some tears in his eyes. His sadness for the loss of his child was balanced. He did not break down into weeping and sorrow. When they questioned the Prophet he replied saying,

$$\text{تدمع العين ويحزن القلب ولا نقول إلا ما يرضي ربنا إنا بك يا إبراهيم لمحزونون}$$

The eye is to have tears and the heart is to be sad, and we say nothing except that pleases our Lord and we are sad about your loss, Ibrahim.

Prophet Muhammad Hadith [4]

One day the Prophet gave his companions great advice on how to control emotions when angry:

إذا غضب احدكم وهو قائم فليجلس، فإن ذهب عنه الغضب وإلا فليضطجع

If one of you is angry while standing, he should sit down, and if he is still angry he should lie down.

Prophet Muhammad Hadith [5]

Balanced Life

Islam is a balanced way of life. It is more than just acts of worship. It is a complete system for living one's life to gain success in this life and the hereafter. The Prophet (peace be upon him) once drew for his companions a line in the sand, showed them a straight path in the middle of branched paths on both sides, and commanded them to follow the straight path which is in the middle.

A Muslim youth life will be balanced between studying, playing, working and fulfilling errands, all with the intention of worshipping Allah (glory be to Him) to gain His pleasure.

5

Prime Examples of Patience
Reflections from the Past

وَآتَاكُم مِّن كُلِّ مَا سَأَلْتُمُوهُ وَإِن تَعُدُّواْ نِعْمَتَ اللّهِ لاَ تُحْصُوهَا إِنَّ الإِنسَانَ لَظَلُومٌ كَفَّارٌ

Ibrahim (14:34)

And [always] does He give you something out of what you may be asking of Him; and should you try to count God's blessings, you could never compute them. [And yet,] behold, man is indeed most persistent in wrongdoing, stubbornly ignorant.

Meaning of Quranic Parable (14:34)

Connect these great stories of patience on the left with the main characters on the right…

My dear father do what you have been commanded, with the will of Allah, you will find me from among the patient	Muhammad
No leave them, should among their offspring rise submitters to Allah	Ibrahim
He went off in anger, imagining that We shall not punish him, but he cried through the darkness that none has the right to be worshipped but You Allah, glorified and exalted	Ismail
My dear father peace be upon you, I will make supplication to my Lord, indeed he has been kind to me	Zakaryia
He said you will find me with the will of Allah highly patient, and will not be disobedient to you	Maryum
My Lord indeed my bones have become feeble and grey hair has spread on my head, and I have never been unblest in my supplication to you	Musa
And the pains of child birth drove her to the trunk of the palm tree and she said, "Would that I have died before this, and had been forgotten and out of sight"	Younis

Arabic Terms

Al-	The
Al-Anbiya	The Prophets
Al-Anfal	The Spoils of War
Al-Baqara	The Cow
Al-Haleem	The Clement
Al-Imran	The Family of Imran (Mary's family)
Al-Kahf	The Cave
Allah	Arabic name for the Creator of the universe
Al-Muminun	The Believers
Al-Nahl	The Bee
Al-Ra'ad	The Thunder
Al-Raheem	The Merciful

Al-Rahman	The Compassionate
Al-Saboor	The Patient
Al-Sajdah	The Prostration
Al-Tur	The mountain Tur
Asr	Afternoon
Ayah	Parable or sign; Verse of the Quran
Ayat	Plural of ayah
Ayoub	Job (peace be upon him)
Duaa	Supplication
Dunya	Life on this earth
Fajr	Dawn
Glory be to Him	Subhano Wa Ta'ala, means glory be to Allah
Hadith	A statement or saying by the Prophet Muhammad
Halal	Permissible
Haram	Sacred, or not allowed, forbidden
Ibrahim	Abraham (peace be upon him)
Islam	Submission
Ismail	Ishmael (peace be upon on him)
Janaba	State of impurity when one needs to have a full shower, an example is after wet dreams
Jannah	Paradise, The Garden, The eternal abode of the believers
Makrooh	Disliked, not recommended
Maryum	Mary (peace be upon her)
Masjid	Mosque
Morabata	Steadfastness

Mosabara	Endurance
Mubah	Neutral, allowed
Muhammad	The last messenger and prophet of Allah
Musa	Moses (peace be upon him)
Muslim	A believer who submits to Allah and believes in Muhammad
Nasheed	Poem
Nooh	Noah (peace be upon him)
Peace be upon him	An Islamic greeting of peace
Quran	The final message revealed by Allah to mankind
Sabr	Patience
Shaytan	Satin, the devil
Taqwa	Piety towards Allah, Fear from the punishment of Allah, a shield between one and the hell-fire
Tasabor	Perseverance
Yaqub	Jacob (peace be upon him)
Younis	Jonah (peace be upon on him)
Youssef	Joseph (peace be upon him)
Zakaryia	Zakaria (peace be upon him)

Learn & Read More

Hadith References

[1] Hadith of the Prophet, narrated by Abi Horayrah; Ahmed, Abu Dawood and Tirmithi.

[2] Hadith of the Prophet, narrated by Omar Ibn Al Khatab; Bukari (853, 2416, 2419, 2600, 4892, 4904, 6719), Muslim (1829), Abu Dawood (2928), Tirmithi (1705) and Ahmed (2/5, 54).

[3] Hadith of the Prophet, narrated by Abu Musa Al-Asharai, Bukhari (7378) and Muslim (2804).

[4] Hadith of the Prophet, narrated by Anas Ibn Malik, Ali Ibn Abi Talib, among others; Abu Dawood (3126), Al-Jama'a (2931), also in Ibn-i Sa'd's, Tabaqat v.1, p.131-144.

[5]   Hadith of the Prophet, narrated by Abi Thar; Ahmed, Abu Dawood, Ibn Hayan, Al-Albani (3/180).

Other References

The Holy Quran

Ibn Qayyim Al- Jawziyyah, "The Provision of the Patient, and the Treasure of the Thankful", عدة الصابرين وذخيرة الشاكرين, (Arabic), Abridged, Al-Maktabah Al-Asrayah, Beirut, Lebanon, 2003.

Muhammad Mohsen Khan, "Summarized Sahih Al-Bukhari", Arabic English, Maktaba Dar us-Salam, Riyadh, Saudi Arabia, 1994.

Didan Abdulrahman Al-Sayeed, "Manners of a Muslim When Angry", آداب ما يفعله المسلم إذا غضب, (Arabic), http://www.alukah.net/

John Hammond, Ralph Keeney and Howard Raiffa, "Smart Choices", Broadway Books, 1999.

Aatif Shams, "Don't Be Sad", لا تحـــــزن, (Arabic), http://www.attef.org/

Abu Aziz Hassan Bin Noor Al-Maroo'ai, "The Authentic Compilation of the Names and Attributes", الجامع الصحيح فى الأسماء والصفات, (Arabic), Dar Al-Iman, Alexandria, Egypt.

ILIA Leadership Development Programs

info@islamicleadership.org – www.islamicleadership.org

If you wish to bring one of these programs to your local community please contact us at the email above.

General Available Programs

Youth Leadership Development
Teacher Classroom Leadership
Parents and Adults – Teen Communications
Inmate Transitioning
Strategic Business Planning
Enterprise Architecture Analysis and Design
Non-profit Fundraising and Development
Project Excellence for Islamic Non-Profits

Youth Leadership Development Programs

Adult – Teen Communications
Purification
Leadership Traits
Project Management

www.ingramcontent.com/pod-product-compliance
Lightning Source LLC
Chambersburg PA
CBHW041546220426
43665CB00002B/46